About the Author

Howard L. Siskind is an accountant, musician, performer, songwriter, photographer, artist and author. He holds degrees in business and psychology. This is Howard's first book. He has twelve original published songs and is in the studio weekly as he continues to write and record. He created, directed and starred in a short video documentary entitled *The Making of Dance with Me* about one of his songs. He has played lead guitar in the rock band "Stillwaters" for more than forty-five years. Howard does his best song and book writing while practicing his guitar, driving alone in his car, on vacations or traveling on an airplane or bus. He is currently working on a follow-up to *Honabeats Says: Crazy Words!* and a medieval fantasy action novel based on the storyline of an original song. Howard lives in Annapolis, Maryland, USA with his wife, Karen, and daughter, Sarah.

Honabeats Says:
Crazy Words!

Howard L. Siskind, Karen L. Siskind & Sarah J. Siskind

Honabeats Says: Crazy Words!

Nightingale Books

NIGHTINGALE PAPERBACK

A CIP catalogue record for this title is available from the British Library.
ISBN 978-1-83875-406-8

Nightingale Books is an imprint of
Pegasus Elliot MacKenzie Publishers Ltd.
www.pegasuspublishers.com

First Published in 2022
Nightingale Books
Sheraton House Castle Park
Cambridge England
Printed & Bound in Great Britain

Dedication

For my loved ones,
For the future,
Remember me.
Phyllis O. Siskind

Acknowledgements

This book has been more than thirty years in the making! I would like express my deepest appreciation to my wife, Karen, and daughter, Sarah. They both provided the fun words included in this book and also helped with creative ideas and editing. I want to acknowledge Jonny Trappe. Because of his artistic talents, I finally had a book to show family, friends and to present to prospective publishers. I'd also like to recognize Julian Earle who helped me with the development of the Honabeats character. Special thanks to Robert H. Deluty who advised me with editing and numerous new author questions. Additional thanks for their support, insights and suggestions to Bill Thompson, Richard Meade, Diane Meade, Jay Meade, the staff of Quality Signs & Engraving, Inc., Cheryl Schnoor Hill, Frances Costello, Brynne Miller, Stacy Block Sutton, Michael Earle, Douglas Schenker (deceased), Margaret Benshaw and Lynn Schwartz. Finally, I would like to thank Pegasus Elliot Mackenzie Publishers for believing in me and all that is possible for Honabeats!

Shhh... Be very quiet... Honabeats is sleeping upstairs, at the end of the hallway.

An _izard is a Lizard without the “L”.
The “L” dropped off when the Lizard fell!

For your b_ast-off to be swift, you'll need
the "L" for lots of lift!

When the light turns g_een, it’s time to go.
Just remember the “R” doesn’t go on the road!

When you’re searching for “A”nother, don’t look for the cow, she has an “U”dder!

Add _oins to your crown to
straighten it proud!

MUTE

Turn your phone to m“U”te, to get over the m“O”at!

If _ellow is “Y”ellow, then Honabeat’s treat, is a yellow banana that’s good to eat!

If the _airy is going to fly, she'll need the
"F" to lift her high.

The word BLUE can be scary too.
Just drop the “L” and blue becomes “BOO!!!”

RRR!

A hai_cut is a haircut without the “R”,
the “R” is for the pirate whose favorite
word is “ARRR!!!”

ROAR!!!

For your sc_eam to be heard by all far away, the “R” must be as loud as the lion can say, “ROAR!!!”

Shhh... You're getting too loud, it's time to calm down. We don't want to wake Honabeats, still sleeping upstairs at the end of the hallway.

A musician with "US" plays a guitar and a harp. A magician with "AG" pulls a rabbit from his hat.

If you mix the two together, you may accidentally get, a m"UG"ician pulling a drum from a hat!

It is almost time for Honabeats to wake!
So, how are we going to get to his room?
The choices are two, or maybe three. It depends
on the second letter in the word we take!

If we choose “L”, then we use the e“L”evator!
If we choose “S”, then we use the e“S”calator!
But, the CrAzY WoRd is the fastest of the three,
We’re going to ride the e“LS”cavator!

We're almost to Honabeats' room...

A
B
C

Hi, I’m Honabeats!
I’ve been awake and with you the entire time!

CPSIA information can be obtained
at www.ICGtesting.com
Printed in the USA
BVHW092308300422
635809BV00015B/333